From the End to the Beginning

Preparation for a marriage based on biblical principles

Pavla King-Johnson

From the End to the Beginning

Cover Design by Pavla King-Johnson

Copyright © 2021, 2025 Pavla King-Johnson

Published in United Kingdom by Excel Life Publishing.

All rights reserved.

This book is protected under the copyright laws. This book may not be copied or reprinted for commercial gain or profit. The use of short quotations or occasional page copying for personal or group study is permitted and encouraged. Permission will be granted upon request.

For more titles from this author see

www.iampkj.com

www.iampkj.company.site

www.excellifepublishing.com

Published by Excel Life Publishing

ISBN: 978-1-78650-019-9 (Paperback)
         978-1-78650-020-5 (eBook)

All Scripture quotations, unless otherwise indicated, taken from the New King James Version®. Copyright © 1982 by Thomas Nelson. Used by permission.

Dedication

To all my sisters in Christ
who chose to walk
in the Spirit
and
be led by the Spirit.
in
time of singleness.

Walking in the Spirit

I say then: Walk in the Spirit, and you shall not fulfil the lust of the flesh. For the flesh lusts against the Spirit, and the Spirit against the flesh; and these are contrary to one another so that you do not do the things that you wish. But if you are led by the Spirit, you are not under the law.

Now the works of the flesh are evident, which are adultery, fornication, uncleanness, lewdness, idolatry, sorcery, hatred, contentions, jealousies, outbursts of wrath, selfish ambitions, dissensions, horseflesh, murders, drunkenness, revelries, like; of which I tell you beforehand, just as I also told you in time past, that those who practice such things will not inherit the kingdom of God. But the fruit of the Spirit is love, joy, peace, longsuffering, kindness, goodness, faithfulness, gentleness, and self-control. Against such, there is no law. And those who are Christ's have crucified the flesh with its passions and desires. If we live in the Spirit, let us also walk in the Spirit.

Galatians 5:16-25

From the End to the Beginning

Table of Contents

From the End to the Beginning xi

Chapter 1: How do you enjoy yourself in the presence of God 1

Chapter 2: For how long should I stay single????? 20

Chapter 3: Who is my godly man? 39

Chapter 4: Where is my godly man? 51

Chapter 5: Meaning of Agape Love 53

Chapter 6: Trust the Lord and be still (waiting time) 60

Chapter 7: How do I know my time has come? 67

From the End to the Beginning

In this book, I will show you how to enjoy yourself in a time of singleness.

When I asked God what a book would be about, what I must write down, and which specific points I had to highlight, the Lord said to me: firstly, teach them to focus on Me. Teach them to seek Me first (**Matthew 6:33**). Tell them that their peace, love, and all things for what they are looking for come from Me.

> **I am the way, the truth, and the life. (John 3:16)**
>
> As we know, everything is about Him. What we must do is just invite God into our lives and let Him help us and lead us in His ways. Without God, we can do nothing, but with God, all things are possible (Matthew 19:26)

In this book, I will focus on preparation for a healthy relationship and marriage.

Firstly, you must learn how to have a personal relationship with God and learn how to connect with Him.

Jesus has spoken with His disciples about Helper, who will send in His name to them to teach them all things. His name is the Holy Spirit.

It is the same Holy Spirit – Spirit of God which dwelled in them will dwell in you and teach you all things.

A good relationship with God means to spend time with Him. If you cannot find time for God and yourself, how do you want to invest your time into a relationship with your partner?

The name of this book, From the End to the Beginning, is a true example of my will and not God's will.

That is why I am here to help you from the Beginning to the End.

The big mistake that we face in relationships today is running without learning.

We focus on the end of the story, but we forget the purpose of the story. 'We want right now a godly man, happy relationship, marriage, and family, but no one has learned how to come there.

The purpose of this book is to help you and navigate you, for do not waste your time as I did.

Moses wasted many years to take His people to the Promised Land, and why? Disobedience: God gave us a chose to follow Him so then we can occupant our land.

Learning is not wasting time; it is investing time. Invest your time in learning, preparing, and growing.

As I passed through many things, I realised how many years I wasted for foolishness.

I had to come back from the end and start learning from the beginning how to walk with God.

He transformed me, cleaned me, and corrected me, but there was also something behind seeing what I did not see.

God has much more in store for us, as we cannot imagine. This transformation and learning time has been the most valuable time ever. I spent intimate time with God like never before. He showed me, in the time of pain, that He has the power to twist it for my good and for His glory.

His Mighty presence takes me to another level of love and surrendering.

We are His beloved daughters in Christ, and He uses us to help one another for His glory. It is my pleasure to help you, serve you on your journey of singleness, and take you through a few steps.

God does not come to confuse us but help us. He is not the God of confusion.

Do not waste your time. My wasted time has been turning from bad to good according to His purpose, which is to encourage you and say, "It is not a time for you to waste your time. Saying again, it is not a time for you to waste your time.

Take notes and pen, call upon the Holy Spirit, and let us grow together step by step.

When we think we are ready to settle down and think that we know everything, suddenly, it is not true. Our flesh may cry out saying; You are ready, but are you ready in the spirit? Do you want to step into the relationship because of our Spirit? Truly, ask yourself.

It is important to know which season you are in. Is it the season of marriage or preparation, or are you in the season of healing, transforming, the season of forgiveness......?

We miss big understanding when we are coming trough seasons.

Not every season is a time of marriage.

Do not let your enemies steal your faith and future. No enemies can steal your future, destroy your relationship, or let you give up if you do not give them power.

Example:

Hammer has the power to break, destroy, and kill, but without your power, it cannot do anything. You are just the only one who gives power to Hummer. Without you, it cannot move. ,

Become a builder of your future, not a destroyer. Take your hammer to build, not to destroy. How to build your future is about how much you want to invest. As much you invest, so much you will build.

As much time you invest in build – so much you will grow – so much knowledge you will take, and many more enemies you will overcome.

To overcome our spiritual enemies, we need knowledge and spiritual growth, which we can freely consume from our living bread. (John 6:51)

It is so easy for enemies to overcome you if your spirit is weak. That's why it is important to pray for wisdom that comes from our Father in heaven.

Why do we need wisdom? Example:

We want a beautiful car, but we do not know how to drive a car because we do not have a driver's license, right?

Then your car is taken away. Why? Because you have been driving without a driver's license, you must also pay a big penalty. (ex. Heart-broken)

When things look like you have lost everything, you will come back from the end to the beginning to learn step by step how to drive a car, get a driver's license, and have your dream car.

And this is a human problem. We want everything right now, without knowledge, learning, growing.

We like to take easier and faster way and if that is possible, for free.

But this is not how God works. It is not His way; this is a way for unbelievers, but as we are one body in Christ, we should follow God's ways. They are higher than our ways. As we know, things in this world are not cheap. They are more valuable than all gold in the world.

Being in spirit means also walking in the Spirit. Growing in the spirit takes time, patience, and hard work.

You must pay a high price and pay attention, sacrifice things, and take not just for free but also freely give.

God's way is valued because you are valued by Him.

Do not lose your value for man, but use your value for God.

Easier ways are always a way of death, but hard work is the way of life.

The same principles are figured in our relationships, marriages, and business acts.

Who wants to take it for free without any investment is like a man who has already lost at all.

But those who invest in such time, patience, and obedience are like a man who already wins.

Read as an example **(Matthew 7:24-27 or Lukas 6:46-49)**

Do not give up just because things take time; remember, it is not on your time, but God's time. It is not a waste of time but is an investment for your future.

Jesus wants you to focus on Him, to call upon His name and say:

``Dear Lord Jesus Christ, I know that I am a sinner. I ask you to forgive me and cleans me from my sins. I believe You died for me and rose from the dead on the third day. I turn from my sins, and I invite You to come into my heart and my life. I accept You, Lord Jesus Christ, as my Saviour, my God, and I believe that You set me free from all my sins, and my name is written now in Your book of life. Amen

His desire is to be with you and speak with you all the time. He is giving you the opportunity to be the best of yourself and get the best for you.

Not because we deserve it but because He loves us.

Do you know the story about the Heavenly Kingdom? It is like the mustard seed.

It is the smallest seed. Takes time to grow, but when he grows, he is bigger and stronger than another.

The same is true with us. Takes time to grow in the spirit, take time to grow, but at the end of the day, we are stronger in faith. Then we can do all things trough Christ who strength us: read: **(Philippians 4:13)**

Chapter One

How do you enjoy yourself in the presence of God

The questions are:

    Do you love yourself?
    Do you know God and His nature?
    Do you care about yourself?
    It is truly important to be honest with your answers.
    If your answer is yes, well done, and I am truly proud of you.

From my experience, I can say I have been blind, or I just do not want to see the truth, but the point is you must be serious if you want to move forward. You cannot come into a relationship with a man without loving yourself, without knowing how to enjoy yourself and how to care about yourself.

It is not working like that. Do not get me wrong now. I talk about relationships from a biblical perspective, for people of faith who decided to follow Christ, do things right, and follow the biblical principles. So, do not be angry with God because your last relationship did not work, and you complain to God over and over: why did He take him out of your life? Why did this happen to me? I am ready, and he was best for me... Why God? Really?

STOP to COMPLAINING!

Do you think you know what is best for you?

Do you think that you are ready for marriage, but you mess up things around?

Be honest and ask yourself: Will you marry yourself?

I know it sounds bad, but just God knows what and who is best for you.

So please, do not complain when God closes a door, but rejoicing for something better to come.

He knows when you are ready, He loves you, He knows you, He wants you to take care of yourself, He wants simply good for you. Be glad and rejoice that His desires are to prepare you to be a perfect woman for the perfect man.

So, Let's Go
Back To The Beginning.

Having enough time for God is truly important.
You must first and always focus on God.
You must trust Him and love Him (Proverbs 3:5-6).

Firstly, find God, then man. Before you come into a relationship with man, build a relationship with God.

If you do not know Him, you do not know what the meaning of true love is. (About which I will speak later.)

To find true love – you should find God.

God is love. Who lives in love lives in God, and God lives in him. You cannot love someone if there is not love in you.

Do you
love yourself?

Ask God. I am not joking.

All my life, I thought that I loved myself, but when my heart was broken, I realised that it was not true.

Of course, I came to the Lord, and I asked Him; I questioned Him if this was necessary.

Do You hate me, Lord? Haven't you forgiven me?

And He said: It was necessary because you hate yourself and you still haven't forgiven yourself.

I already have forgiven you; I paid the price for you.

If you are not happy as a single person, you can't be happy in a relationship either.

A relationship is not about happiness. It is about joy, which comes from the Lord and not from man.

The question is: How can you love yourself while still holding back to the past, not being able to forgive yourself? How can I say that I know God while thinking that He didn't forgive me or hate me?

No, no, no! Those voices and questions are not coming from God.

Those toughs are the signs that some doors should be closed, but some are still open. Something must be shut down because negative toughs are not coming from God. It can mean that our spirit is weak, and lack of knowledge makes us struggle in many areas of our live, especially in relationships. An open door can invite our enemies and give them power to control our life and destiny.

Jesus said: Come to Me, all *you* who labour and are heavy laden, and I will give you rest. Take My yoke upon you and learn from Me, for I am gentle and lowly in heart, and you will find rest for your souls. For My yoke *is* easy, and My burden is light." **(Matthew 11:28-30)**

He is calling you and knocking on your door, waiting for you to open the door for Him.

Do not let Him wait; invite Him into your life, sit with Him, speak with Him, and ask Him for strength and a heart able to forgive others and yourself.

He will take all your worries from you; He will give you rest, and He will set you free.

Being free is a wonderful gift from His grace.

It means to be free from stress, weakness, troubles, and worries, free from angriness and depression....

Being free means also enjoying yourself, loving yourself, and rejoicing in everything you do because every season, month, and day is created by God to praise His name.

HOW CAN WE REJOICE IN EVERYTHING ALL THE TIME?

- Stop focusing on things from the world.
- Write down your golds and act on them.
- Enjoy your hobbies.
- Spend time with your family and friends.
- Sacrifice your free time to help another...

Remember that you are doing everything that you are doing for God.

As Jesus said (Matthew 25:35-45)

'For I was hungry, and you gave Me food; I was thirsty, and you gave Me drink; I was a stranger, and you took Me in; I *was* naked, and you clothed Me; I was sick, and you visited Me; I was in prison, and you came to Me.'

'Then the righteous will answer Him, saying, 'Lord, when did we see You hungry and feed *You*, or thirsty and give *You* drink? When did we see You a stranger and take *You* in, or naked and clothe *You?* Or when did we see You sick or in prison and come to You?' And the King will answer and say to them, 'Assuredly, I say to you, inasmuch as you did *it* to one of the least of these My brethren, you did *it* to Me.' "Then He will also say to those on the left hand, 'Depart from Me, you cursed, into the everlasting fire prepared for the devil and his angels: for I was hungry and you gave Me no food; I was thirsty, and you gave Me no drink; I was a stranger, and you did not take Me in, naked and you did not clothe Me, sick and in prison and you did not visit Me.' "Then they also will answer Him, saying, 'Lord, when did we see You hungry or thirsty or a stranger or naked or sick or in prison, and did not minister to You?' Then He will answer them, saying, 'Assuredly, I say to you, inasmuch as you did not do *it* to one of the least of these, you did not do *it* to Me.'

When you come into a relationship, it can be too late for it.

When children come, you will most probably have less time for your hobbies, dreams, goals, and, in general, yourself. It is a great starting point for depression and stress. It is not unusual at this time to constantly complain about what you have lost, what you have missed, and what you wish would have been done before marriage.

And what can happen then? You can destroy your destiny, relationship, and the future.

This does not have to happen if you choose the right way to follow.

Do not bring any unhealthy habits or bondage from the past into your new relationship if you don't want to destroy it.

Surely, this happens for reasons as are:

1)
- Lack of knowledge.
- Unloving yourself.
- Unforgiveness.
- Lack of knowledge about God.

OR:

2)

- Making your partner your Idol

Another reason behind destroyed relationships is making your partner your idol.

Yes, your idol.

Sis, I am telling you the truth –idealising your spouse, marriage, or anything else is dangerous. And it can kill your relationship.

And as we know from the Bible, God is jealous God.

In (Exodus 20:3) God speaks about having no other gods - idols before Me. It means to love something or someone more than Him.

Do not spend more time focusing on your partnership, marriage, or job than on God.

He is our only one, first love, and true love. As we can see in the Bible (**Revelation 2:4**), the author says that we have forgotten our first love. We must seek His face first. Where is not God welcome, there is not blessing also.

Remember: As He gave, He can take away.

The reason why our spouse is taken away from us is simply because it is not good for us, or because we started our relationship the wrong way and not from God`s way, or they come from our will and not from God's will. When any issue comes, sadly, then we turn back to God.

And why? Simply because we need His help. We should understand that we always need His help, not just when troubles arise.

For this reason, we need to seek the Lord before the troubles come.

We must seek Him every day, all the time. Everything that we have comes from Him.

We must glorify His name because He is a good Father.

We are thinking that all that we need is the man and his love. When we are receiving love, we forget about God. We think that we have everything.

Let's say being in love or being loved does not mean we have everything that we need in a relationship.

It's much more than to be loved by a man. We should know that loving one another means trusting and respecting one another.

START BUILDING
YOUR RELATIONSHIP ON:

- Trust

- Respect

Where there is no respect and trust, there is no love. The same principles are with God.

You can't just take it. If you struggle with selfishness, it's better for you to take your time and stay single until you don't die in yourself. A healthy relationship is about serving, sharing, and so on.

It is not 'me' anymore, but 'us'.

For those reasons, we need to take time for our-selves and grow in the spirit.

We need to learn how to have self-control and patience and how to love, forgive, and help one another.

Come pure into the relationship; don't bring old habits with heaviness, angriness, stress, worry, and unforgiveness.

Run away from the old ways, change your shoes, let God anointed your head, clean your hands, and change your mind.

Ask the Holy Spirit for help (John 14: 16,17)

The Bible teaches us to be one in Christ as He and Father are one.

What does it mean for you to be one? When you are born again, you receive the Holy Spirit; God`s Spirit lives in you.

If you still do not like yourself, you need a breakthrough or healing. Find the root of why you do not like yourself, and let the Holy Spirit help you.

> **Being in Christ means love and light should be in us, and where the light is, there is no darkness. We should bring our light everywhere we go to everyone who's in need; then, people will see that Christ is within us and His light shines upon us. (Isaiah 60:1).**

Love and enjoy yourself. Eat His flash and drink His blood daily.

Stay pure and humble yourself before God, and He will direct your path. Obey His voice, and He will lead you and teach you His ways.

Stop listening to other unbelievers telling you that you shall do this and not do that because you are boring, different, or whatever reason it is.

Yes, we may look like a bed, but we are different. Hallelujah Praise the Lords for being different.

We are no longer interested in man's will but in the will of God. Stop caring about what others say or what they think about you. Care about what God can see and what He thinks about you. That is what matters most.

Your choice is just in your hands.

You must decide which way you want to go.

Choose your destiny NOW.

God gives us a choice; He gives us a choice
(Matthew 16:25)

Make sure you ask God if anything in your heart or life requires forgiveness or breakthrough.

Do not think that you are fine and that you know everything because it's just Him who knows.

You can lie to yourself, but you cannot hide anything from His eyes.

The question is:

Do you truly love yourself?

The bible says: love your neighbours as yourself
(Mark 12:30-31).

Lastly, do not forget to care about yourself.

Remember, your body is the Holy Temple, so you should stay humble and pure but also stay away from an unhealthy lifestyle. Taking care of your body is honouring God. Walking like Jesus is being like Him.

If you do so – Congratulations!
We can move to another level now.

Notes:

From the End to the Beginning

John 3:16

For God so loved the world that He gave His only begotten Son, that whoever believes in Him should not perish but have everlasting life.

Psalm 139:14

I will praise the Lord, for I am fearfully and wonderfully made.

If there is anything that must be forgiven or anyone who you must forgive, write it all down. Then ask God to forgive you and to give you and people your heart the heart able to forgive.

Prayer

Dear Father

SPEAK WITH GOD.

Write down everything that you are struggling with (worries, stresses, pains, angriness, fears, jealousy, selfishness, pride, etc) and ask God to clean, change, and deliver you form that.
He will do it as He promised!

Remind Him of His promises trough reading the scripture!

- _____
- _____
- _____
- _____
- _____
- _____
- _____
- _____
- _____

Find the time and worship Him,
praise Him, pray to Him, and read His word.

What are your goals for this year?
Or another 5 or 10 years?
Write them down and take the action!

My goals

- _____
- _____
- _____
- _____
- _____
- _____
- _____
- _____
- _____
- _____

What are your hobbies?
What do you like to do in your free time?
Write them down one by one and follow them.
Be available for your friends and family.
Ask them if they need any help, and pray for them.
Be fruitful!!

Things I love to do (My hobbies)

- _____
- _____
- _____
- _____
- _____
- _____
- _____
- _____
- _____

Chapter Two

For how long should I stay single?????

It's a good question.

One of the keys to a godly relationship is to be spiritually healthy.

We are all unique, and before starting a relationship, we must focus on our own preparation process.

What is a preparation process?

It is a time, as mentioned before, for learning in the time of singleness.

Preparation time to

1. Know your gifts and talents.
2. Know who you are in Christ.
3. Know the purpose of your life.

All Christians who have been born again have a purpose and play a part in God's plan for the earth.

And so, by God's grace, we all received Spiritual gifts. Also, we have talents that we are called to use for God's glory.

Gifts and talents are two different things:

Spiritual gifts (from the Holy Spirit) are:
1. Ministry
2. Manifestation
3. Motivational

The ministry gift (God's work) is the one to serve others and meet their needs.

And there are differences of administration, but the same Lord.' **(1 Corinthians 12:5)**

Those are:
- Apostles
- Prophets
- Evangelists
- Pastors
- Teachers
- Helpers

The manifestations gifts are:
- A message of wisdom
- A massage of knowledge
- Faith
- Gift of healing
- Miraculous power

- Prophecy
- Distinguishing between spirits
- Speaking in different kinds of tongues
- The interpretation of tongues

Motivational gifts are:
- Prophesying
- Serving
- Teaching
- Encouraging
- Giving
- Leading
- Showing mercy

We have Spiritual gifts as well as talents.

Our merciful God blessed all of us with Spiritual gifts. Many of us have one, and some have more, but all these gifts come from the same Spirit (**1 Corinthians 12:7-11**), and we are called to use them.

God's plan is to use us to finish His plan on the Earth. We are part of His purpose.

Do you know what plans God has for you?

It does not matter how old you are or who you were in the past.

To be part of His plan and complete the purpose of the plan He has for you, you should obey His voice.

I am not saying that by disobeying, you will lose His love or care, but you will mess up things around you. When you feel disappointed or lost, it can be because you are not what God called you to be or you do not do what He called you to do for what He has created you.

You are unique – you are shaped, for some specific reason, for His time, such as this, to fulfil His purpose in the earth.

Coming into the relationship without knowing your purpose is like going nowhere. Once God reveals to you what His plan for your future is, follow that. It can take time, but everyone who seeks Him will find Him.

When you come into the relationship, you should know your priorities and standards.

The main thing you will be focused on is Jesus and His will. Will it be like that, or will it be you and your own will?

In the book of Genesis 29, we can see the difference between our will and God's will.

Genesis 29 speaks about Jacob and his two wives - Leea and Rachel.

He loved Rachel, and he had been working for 7 years to marry her. But he got her sister, Leea, as a wife because she was older.

And because he loved Rachel, he worked another 7 years to marry her also.

The thing is that God's will was Leea, not Rachel.

Rachel was Jacob's will, not God's will.

As you can see in Matthew 1:2, the genealogy of Christ comes from Leea and her son Judas. Read Genesis 29 for yourself to understand a story and what I try to say if you do not understand.

Because of fulfilling his (Jacob's) own will, Jacob introduced hatred, jealousy, and pain between sisters. He could avoid it if he listened to God. God never desires polygamy, divorce, or cheating.

I have been facing all these ways of disobedience. However, now I've learned from my mistakes, and I know the plan which He has for me. One of His plans is to encourage you and to bring you on the right way – a way of winner as we are all in Christ.

> **God has a plan for you. His plan is for you to prosper, not to do harm. His plan is for hope and for the future (Jeremiah 29:11)**

TALENTS

When we were born, we were born with talents. Everyone has different talents, such as music, dance, creativity, etc.

God gave us so many talents according to our ability.

But with spiritual gifts, it is different. We are not born with them. We must deserve them and then receive them as a gift from God after we are born again.

Being born again is a process.

It takes time.

Many of us may still not understand what it means to be born again. The Bible teaches us when we are born again, we are new creatures in Christ.

> **Old things are passing away, behold, and all things become new (2 Corinthians 2:12).**
>
> **This means that God will give you a new heart and new spirit as He promised (Ezekiel 36:26).**

You will be cleaned from your sins, and then you will be ready to receive His spiritual gifts.

As we are born again, God will prepare us and shape us to use our talents and spiritual gifts for His glory.

Before we were born, He knew us.

He separated us from the darkness to the light in this world.

> **He gives as the opportunity to walk and run with Him (Ephesians 2:10).**
>
> **He has a plan for us, for our future, to glorify His name on earth.**
>
> **Ask God to reveal to you the purpose of your life and His perfect will for you. (Matthew 7:7)**

Be confident that He will provide a way for it.

Ask Him to give you everything that you will need.

He calls you to use your spiritual gifts and talents wherever His name can be glorified. Keeping your talents for yourself is like a parable (**Matthew 25: 14-30**) when the Lord explains about multiplying your talents. Otherwise, you will lose what you have.

> **He calls us to be a good steward. (1 Peter: 4-10).**

KNOWING WHO YOU ARE

What are your dreams and goals?

To complete your dreams and goals, you need to have faith.

Without faith, your dreams and goals will not manifest. They will fail.

Use your faith to achieve your dreams and goals.

All of us have dreams or goals.

Something that is burning in our hearts.

We can dream about our destiny, marriage, husband, future, career, or goals to have our own business at a specific time.

Find yourself who you are, and check your values.

Know what the purpose of your life is.

When you feel like a burning fire in your heart in your spirit, it is a calling from God. He puts His desire into your heart. His desire in your heart is yours. It is no longer your will but His will.

> **We should understand that what we want is not always what God wants for us (Isaiah 55:8)**

And not everything we want, we need!

It is not about what we want but what He wants – what is best for us. He is calling you to do things He created you for. He prepared you and shaped you for His best time to use your talent and spiritual gift in your life. To share with others.

> **Do not be afraid because He is with you. He has not given us a spirit of fear but the spirit of power and love and a sound mind (2 Timothy 1:7).**

So don't thing that you are not good enough. You and your talents are special to Him.

Ask God and pray how He can use your talents and gifts and how they can be manifested in your life.

Find the purpose of your life and act. Put a price on you. And let every man want you.

And when they had found Him, they said unto Him, All (man) seek for thee., (Mark 1:37)

Why does all man seek Jesus?
He was holding something valuable.
How big is your value?

Proverb 31 teaches us how to value ourselves as a woman who knows their talents and passions, who is wise and not lazy. The woman who uses her talents for multiplying, so when ``cold time'' comes, she doesn't have to worry.

Be like this woman, and all men will see your value.

Remember that your Father is the King, and you are His princes. He will always help you with everything that's working according to His plan.

Ask God for
- Wisdom
- Strength
- Courage

Ask Him for all the things you need to be like a virtuous woman. Seek Him and His help, and He will give you all that you need and even more.

The price of virtuous woman Proverbs 31

She seventh wool and flax and worketh willingly with her hands. (31:13)

She considereth a field, and buyeth it: with the fruits of her hands, she planthet a vineyard. (31:16)

She perceiveth that her merchandise is good: her candle goeth not out by night (31:18)

She is not afraid of the snow for her household, for all her household is clothed with scarlet. (31:21)

What are your talents? How you can use them? Write them down, pray, and ask God to reveal them to you.

- _____
- _____
- _____
- _____
- _____
- _____
- _____
- _____
- _____
- _____
- _____
- _____

How I can use them:

From the End to the Beginning

What are your Spiritual gifts? Pray and ask God; also you can check on the website:

- _____
- _____
- _____
- _____
- _____
- _____
- _____
- _____
- _____
- _____
- _____
- _____
- _____

Pray to God to connect you with the right people who will help you to grow in Him, and ask Him to bring you to the right places where you can use your Spiritual gifts.

What are your dreams? What is the desire for your future in your heart?
Use this space to write a letter to God.
He will do everything that you desire in your heart according to His will. Remember, pray with faith. Without faith, it is impossible to please God.
Have faith!

Dear Father
My God, my Lord, my Saviour, my everything

_____
_____
_____
_____
_____
_____
_____
_____
_____
_____

From the End to the Beginning

What is the purpose of your Life?
Pray and ask God to reveal to you what it is and how He wants you to use it.
You were born for a purpose in a time like this.

AFFIRMATION

I am a crown of beauty and a royal diadem
in the hand of the Lord.
(Isaiah 62:3-4)

I am more than a conqueror.
(Romans 8:37)

I am a child of God.
(1 John 3:1)

I am His own special treasure.
(Deuteronomy 14:2)

I am a friend of God.
(John 15:15)

I am made in God`s image.
(Genesis 1:27)

I am redeemed.
(Ephesians 1:7)

I am marked with the
seal of the promised Holy Spirit.
(Ephesians 1:13)

I am the salt and light of the world.
(Matthew 5:13-16)

I am an ambassador for God.
(2 Corinthians 5:20)

I am healed.
(Isaiah 53:5)

I am never alone.
(Hebrew 13:5)

I am a new creation.
(2 Corinthians 5:17)

I am accepted.
(Romans 15:7)

I am chosen.
(John15:16)

I am strong.
(Ephesians 6:10)

I am wonderfully made.

(Psalm 139:14)

I am forgiven.

(1 John 2:12)

I am seated in the
heavenly realms with Christ Jesus.

(Ephesians 2:6)

and

I can do all things through
Christ who strengthens me.

(Philippians 4:13)

Chapter Three

Who is my godly man?

Do not try to figurate out how to find a godly man; focus on how to be a godly woman.

No godly man is looking for the ungodly woman, which is like a slanderer addicted to wine (Titus 2:3-4); if you want the best for you, become the best for him. Do you want to be blessed by your partner? Be a blessing for him also.

Especially important is the scripture (Matthew 7:12), where Jesus speaks that everything you want from men, you should do to them as well.

It is not just reading and knowing scripture that is important; it is also applying it to your life and relationship, living by the scripture.

Firstly, you should ask God not to bring a godly man to you but to make a godly woman from you.

Not gold is everything that is shining.

Looking like a goddess does not mean you are godly.

Your beauty comes from the bottom of your heart. It is a fruit of the Holy Spirit which is in you. It is a bigger value than all your necklaces or shoes.

Righteousness and kindness should be the crown on your head, and thereafter, everyone will see how beautiful you are. (1 **Timothy** 9-10).

What does a
godly woman look like?

Godly woman should be like a tree full of fruits.

All fruits have different tastes, different sizes, and different characteristics.

As they grow, their characteristics, colours, taste, and size are change.

When their season comes, we use them to procedure wines, jams, juices, cakes…

Different fruits, different tastes, and different products.

But in the end, they have one thing in common: they were made for the same purpose: for multiplying and for making others happy.

And why?

Their taste is good.

Who tastes them, at once, knows from which tree they are coming.

Someone loves them, and someone hates them.

But we have a choice.

Every good fruit has a few specific characteristics which we can see with a natural and spiritual eye:

Looks good,
smells good, and tastes good.

Those characteristics I will try to explain to you the meaning of a godly woman in the eyes of a man:
- looking
- smelling
- tasting

Three valuable things that men see with natural and spiritual eyes. Spiritual eyes of man

<u>Look good all the time</u>- *Strength and honour are her clothing: and she shall rejoice in time to come to* **(Pr. 31:25)**.

<u>Smell good</u> – meaning the way you speak.

She opened her mouth with wisdom, and in her tongue is the law of kindness. (Pr. 31:26)

<u>Taste good</u> – meaning the way you make things. *She looked well to the ways of her household and ate not the bread of idleness* **(Pr. 31:27)**

> The Bible tells us about who is the woman of noble character in Proverbs 31:10-12

Who can find a virtuous wife?

For her worth is far above rubies. The heart of her husband safely trusts her. So, he will have no lack of gain. She does him good and not evil all the days of her life.

> God made a man (Adam), and He saw it was not good for him to be alone, so he made him a helper - Eva
> (Genesis 2:18)

Many ladies do not know what it means to be a godly woman and helper.

We have been made as helpers, not destroyers.

> Before you come into the relationship, you should accept that man is the head of woman as Christ is the head of man.
> (1 Corinthians 11:3)

You should know that **LOVE** is not a feeling but a **CHOICE**.

Building and showing your Love in:

- Respect **(Ephesians 5:33)**
- Obedience **(Titus 2:5)**
- Support **(Ephesians 5:22-24)**

<u>This is a meaning of love in man's eyes.</u>
- To disagree is better for man to stay alone **(Proverbs 21:19)**
- To agree is to be like a virtuous woman and have her husband's heart trusting **(Proverbs 31:11)**

A man must love his wife as he loves himself.
Protect and save her also. **(Ephesians 5: 25-28)**

Who is a godly woman, and how to become one?

A) Who is a godly woman:
- A woman with a pure heart
- A righteous woman
- A wise woman

B) How to become a godly woman

A woman with a pure heart does things with kindness.
A woman with a pure heart does things with patience.
A woman with a pure heart does things with faith, hope, and love.

A righteous woman is a woman of sound mind.
A righteous woman is a woman of self-control.
A righteous woman is a woman of not judgmental mind.

Wise women will not argue but respect.
Wise women will not be complaining but will obey God's word.
Wise women will not dishonour but serve.

To be a godly woman is a choice.
Ask God to touch your heart and receive the fruit of spirit from Him.
Man's nature is to feel like Man– to be head of house and family, for what he was created.

A man needs to have everything in control.
A man needs a woman to make him feel important.

A man needs a woman who will always support him and respect him.

A man needs a woman who will absolutely trust him.

This means you will leave your life in his hands.
You will submit yourself to him.

As I mentioned before, the head of the woman is her husband.

It is not just mentioned in the New Testament but also in the Old Testament in the book of Genesis when God gave Adam dominion over all creatures on earth. God also commanded man not to eat from the tree of knowledge of good and evil. He didn't speak with a woman; He commanded this to man.

So, when the woman ate from the tree of knowledge, nothing happened, whereas when a man ate, their eyes opened, and God asked the man, 'Where are you?' - He spoke to the man directly, not to the woman or both.

When God saw that they ate from the tree of knowledge, He asked man, why you ate and he said, 'it was a woman you brought to me that gave me an apple to eat.

After that, God spoke with woman.

The point is God gave commandments to man, not woman.

The commandment was broken because of the following:
- Disobedience of God.
- Lack of knowledge.
- A man lets a woman have power over him.

It is so important to understand where we are and why.

From the beginning, God gave us rules and principles. That's why the Bible teaches us who is the head and why.

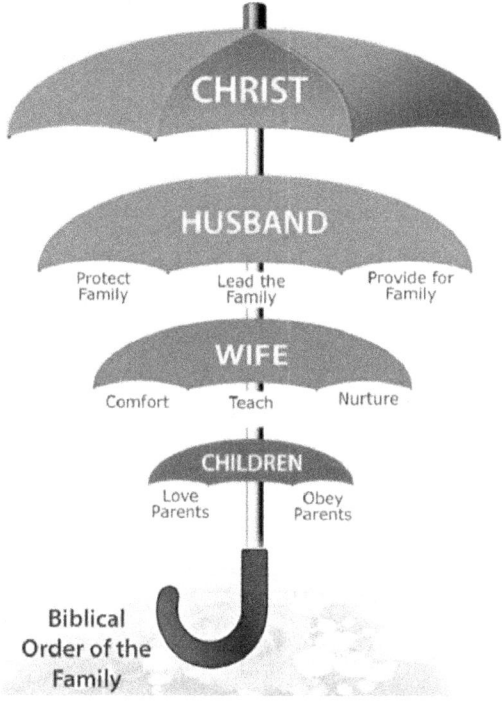

Do not make the same mistake repeatedly.

Every true Christian should understand biblical principles and main rules before jumping into marriage.

Man is created to be the head of a woman – to be leader provider.

To be a leader means to have enough knowledge to lead and provide. To be spiritually highest or on the same level as a woman.

We should learn from the man and not teach them, which is very important. How can you be a man leader and head of your head if you are his teacher? How can he lead if he does not know where he is going? To be in a healthy relationship, make sure that your partner has the same or the highest spiritual knowledge us you have. Make sure that he knows what it means to be a leader provider. Who is he in Christ, what is his purpose, does he have a vision?

He must be a man of vision and prayer. Man fearing God, who fully obeys Him, honours Him and puts Him always first.

Let a man be a man. You should understand that you are not the head of man, but the head of man is Jesus Christ.

When you are taking a position to be a head of man – it means you are taking a position of Christ; you are taking your relationship into your own hands – you become rebellious. Makes sense?

Build your relationship on:

- Principles
- Rules
- Purpose

Prepare yourself before you come to marriage. Use singleness time wisely. Build yourself.

As much you build yourself so much your value will grow. Then God will know which man is matching for you because you will know your value – you will stand and build on principles so then God will know for which kind of man you are looking for.

Most likely, we attract what we are.

Advice: be best of you.

Then, in the book of **(Genesis 2:22, 2:24)** God brought woman to man. Therefore, shall a man leave his father and his mother, and shell cleave unto his wife: and they shell be on flesh.

Remember:
1. God created a man.
2. God gave him dominion over all creatures.
3. God created a woman to be a helper for man.

You are created for a man – your future husband is waiting on you. God will never bring you to the man who is not from Him. So, take action and build yourself.

When you are ready, then God will bring you to your husband, and He will wake him up and open his eyes to see you and recognise you as his wife. **(Genesis 2:21-22)**

He will not bring you to the man if you or he are not ready yet.

As strong as you are in Christ, much stronger will base your relationship.

I hope you got what I am trying to say.

Would you like to be a Godly woman? Women powered by the grace of God, rooted in faith, in powered in love—women with a heart of prayer.

I encourage you to be that woman.

HOW TO BE A GODLY WOMAN?

Write down what you would like your future husband to be like: (Example: fitness body, no drinking, no party man, have self-control, eating healthy, business-minded, caring person, kindly, humble, and so on)

And ask yourself, are you as what you ask him to be?
If not, so start working on yourself or change your note because you should look like his mirror when he sees you.

- _____
- _____
- _____
- _____
- _____
- _____
- _____
- _____
- _____
- _____
- _____
- _____

What are you looking for in your relationship - marriage?

Written down

Chapter Four

Where is my godly man?

Many of us have the same questions. Where is my husband God? Did he lose direction? Did he exist? Is it someone whom I know? Does he know me? Did he pray for me? What is his name, God? When do we meet? I have to find him, or he will find me?

> "He who finds a wife finds a good thing and obtains Favor from the Lord." (Proverbs 18:22)

That is good news, and the answer: he will find you. Chill and relax, but not too much. He will find you, but also you should be seen. He will not find you if you are sitting at home and watching Netflix.

You must be in places to be found.

Be active, volunteering, fellowship with other Christians, do outreach, feed the homeless, pray for people, help others, be creative, go for worship, be involved in your church, do whatever God calls you to do, do it. Be who He calls you to be.

> "But seek the first kingdom of God and His righteousness, and all these things shall be added to you." (Matthew 6:33)

Look at Ruth and Rebekah.... they were not looking to find their husband; they were doing their daily job, and they were found by man in God's timing.

As you look for things for God and live your humble Christian life, God will take you to places to be found by your Boaz.

Be faithful as your heavenly Father is faithful.

Your husband can be anywhere, maybe in a place where you will not expect to meet him, even in a shop, gym, or park. We are still human beings having our hobbies, daily routines, and jobs.

The thing is to be first and always in your Father's business, and rest leave in God's hand.

Stop focusing all the time on where you have to go to be found or what you have to do to be found.

It is ok to take care of yourself as you don't know when you will meet your Boaz, but don't waste time to figure out those things. Because you can't, it will happen; your part is just to focus on God and be ready spiritually so God can lead you and your future husband to meet at the right time.

Chapter Five

Meaning of agape love

God loved the world, that he gave his only begotten son, that whosoever believes in Him should not perish but have an everlasting life. (John 3:16).

Love is divided into 4 types:
1. Storge – empathy
2. Philia – friends
3. Eros – romantic
4. Agape – unconditional God's Love

Imagine the love of God: He loved us before we loved Him; He chose us before we have chosen Him.

Imagine His patience to wait on you until you return to Him; imagine what He must have forgiven; imagine how faithful He is; nothing can't stop Him from loving you. He is so faithful because He knew that one day, you will love Him back.

This is the meaning of Agape- true Love. To have a relationship established on Agape Love, you should first understand what the meaning is.

Remember that He died for us so we can have life. To understand His love, you should know Him not just as your Father and friend but also as your husband. That is what He is, your husband. Speak with Him, listen to Him, do all things with Him and for Him.

It's nice to sing songs I love you Lord and so, but do you really love Him? We are saying a lot of things, but sometimes they are just empty words.

Because if we truly love Him, we will seek Him, and we will not complain but obey Him and trust Him.

Example: some of us, when we say we are in love with someone, we will do anything for that person, right?

We gave him all our time, ourselves, and spent all our money on gifts for someone who never marriage us, someone who left us and forgot about us. We spoke with him, called him, taken care of him. And why? Because we were in love with someone who said I would never leave you; I love you.

In the same way, God sees you – us. He wants for us just good. He knows what is or who is good for you. In the same way, as we want to give or love to someone, He is giving His love to us. Think about what God said: He would never leave us and what He said He means. If we truly love Him in the same way as He does, we will not question Him; we will not complain to Him. But fully trust Him.

Imagine that your loved one will be complaining to you and be angry whit you, don't call you, don't speak with you. How will you feel? Will harm you, right? And why? You didn't do anything wrong; you gave him everything, and he harmed you.

Can you understand now how God feels? Who died for you? He is a real and living God; because we don't see Him, it doesn't mean He is not alive.

He is a jealous God. He wants to make sure that when He brings your spouse into your life, He can fully trust you.

You will remember who your first love is, your beloved.

He must always be in the centre of your life. Doesn't matter what; He will always come first. Not your friend, parents, or husband but Him.

Take time for Him, call His name, worship Him, and give back your love to Him.

Everything will happen at His perfect time. He knows the desire of your heart. He is never late.

Take this time of singleness as an opportunity for you to grow in His perfect love.

Love the Lord with all your heart, with all your mind, with all your soul, and with all your strength (Matthew 22:37)

Be still and know I am your God. **(Psalm 46:10)** He will make way for those who trust and wait on Him... He is a faithful God...

It is God's desire for you to live in harmony in a healthy relationship in love, joy and peace.

Tips to know
before you start dating:

1. Dating with purpose.
2. God's perfect will for you
3. Your calling
4. Purpose of marriage

Dating with purpose

What is dating with purpose? It is a healthy way to find a spouse. Dating with purpose is about to go to meet with your potential future husband.

God's perfect will for you

Ask God to show you His perfect will trough vision.

Your calling

Pray fast and ask God what He calls you to do and how He wants to use you.

He will show you trough Spiritual gifts and talents.

Also, you can use the test: what are your Spiritual gifts on the website below.

www.gifts.churchgrowth.org

Purpose of marriage

Be careful and do not mix the purpose with the vision of marriage.

They are two different meanings.

The vision of marriage can be presented as a picture of how you see yourself as a wife and mum in the future.

> The purpose of marriage is to accomplish God's plan and to use marriage for His glory. As He said, two are better than one. (Ecclesiastes 4:9-10)

Do not lose the main reason for marriage with the idealising vision of marriage. Looking from the wrong perspectives as to what I can lose or what I can take from it, instead of that, ask God how He wants to use your marriage. It is not anymore about you and a beautiful picture of your future family but is much more. God doesn't want you to be married just because He wants to see you happy, but because He needs you, He needs to use you and your husband. He has a plan for you. Do not think about what you can get from it but what you can bring into it.

Describe the meaning of agape love. Use this space to write a letter about the love of God in your life and how God shows you and gives His love to you. How His love manifests in your life.

WHAT IS THE PURPOSE OF YOUR MARRIAGE?

If God has already revealed it to you, write it down and make sure you will fallow it! If you don't know yet, surely you can keep it for later.

_____

_____

_____

_____

_____

Chapter Six

Trust the Lord and be still (waiting time)

> But those who trust in the Lord will find new strength.
> They will soar high on wings like eagles.
> They will walk and not faint (Isaiah 40:31).

No one is saying that the waiting time and preparation time will be easy.

It is pretty much dependent on your obedience and trust. Sometimes, things take the longest time, not because we are growing too slowly but because there are things in the atmosphere shifting around. It's something that we can't see – and usually, this is the hardest time – let's say, testing time- growing time – training time.

> It is a time when we want to give up because we can't see anything – but God working even when we can't see (John 5:17)

> Wait for the Lord to be strong and take heart and wait for the Lord. (Psalm 27:14).

God gives us visions, dreams, desires to meet the right man, to have a blessed family, and all those things. This desire is from the designer. This means you can't fulfil your desire for the relationship without your designer. What we can do is take a step and walk with God and fully trust Him.

> Let the Lord long to be gracious to you; therefore, He will ride you up to show you compassion. For the Lord is a God of justice. Blessed are all who wait for Him (Isaiah 30:18)

TRUST THE LORD:

Look at Abraham and his story. He had been **waiting** and praying for years for his promised son Isaiah, and when God blessed them with a son, what happened later?

God says kill him.

And as we know, Abraham obeyed God's voice and took Isaiah to sacrifice him.

> What I want to show you is trust and obedience. Abraham completely trusted God; he was a friend of God. At that time, Abraham remembered the words that God had spoken to him when he said, look up into the sky and count the stars if you can. That's how many descendants you will have (Hebrews 11:17-20)

Abraham had in his hands just God's promise, nothing visible.

Our big issue is that we say we have just promises from God or just visions, just, dreams from God.

We forget that what we need is faith – trust in Him. We don't need anything else. Just trust the Lord that He will provide in His perfect time.

His words are true, and His promises always come through.

We are not as hypocrites that saying shows us then we will believe. Jesus showed many miracles, and people still don't believe in Him.

We always want more and more. That means there is no trust in us.

That's why things take the longest time, too. I know I can be frustrating but trust God always.

He will show you the small picture or the biggest. He will not show you how to get there.

And this is the main point (testing our trust and faith)

Many of us will not take this walk with Jesus.

Narrow is the gate, and difficult is the way which leads to life, and there are few who find it. (Matthew 7:14)

Remember, when God speaks, He speaks true – He is the true.

Jesus Christ is the same yesterday and today and forever (Hebrews 13:8)

He is not changing.

Waiting time is a truly awesome time of growing in spirit. It is a blessed time with our Father our God; it is a time of learning and teaching His nature and His ways. It is a time of building up a personal relationship with God.

God knows your needs, and He will prepare a place for you.

Speak with Him and ask Him to build a relationship together for your future.

Don't run away from Him to your best friend asking for help or answering your questions; make God Jesus your best friend.

He knows answers to your questions before you ask Him; let Him speak- He always speaks; we just don't listen to Him; let Him help you in every situation.

Don't let others choose your destiny or your future husband; they don't know what is best for you. Of course, take some advice from another, but remember who your first source is. Be dependent on God, not on others.

Ask God to give you a vision and dreams; ask Him to show you a purpose of marriage and His best will for you.

Always ask for confirmation multiple times.

After that, it will come your time. Time to come to your promised land. In a time when you will not expect it. He is never late. He always comes at His perfect time.

Heaven will open, and your cup will overflow, and all your dreams will come true. Our God is an awesome God.

It doesn't matter how big or small your dreams are. Remember, for God is nothing too big or too far.

Don't focus on waiting time for your marriage or future husband...

It is a precious time of trusting process, a time to use everything that you learned from the past and approve into your life.

Focusing on your future husband can destroy many of your blessings. Many people will be sent to your life as a blessing from God to bless you in many areas of your life, but you can lose them if you see all of them as your potential husbands.

No, every man is your future husband. All of them are your brothers. You should see them and treat them as brothers in Christ.

Waiting time is not a time when you are looking for your future husband.

Let God bring you to him in His time. He will find you; do not stress, do not worry, and trust God, and He will make a way.

Obey His voice and all things that you had asked Him in your prayers; He will answer you.

Remember, it is not all about you. God's ways and thoughts are as big as yours. (Isaiah 55:8)

God created Adam and Eva and marriage for a purpose.

It is not just about having a nice wedding party and white dress and having beautiful babies. It's much more.

Waiting season can look like punishment, but it is not. It can be development.

Look at Jacob. His brothers hated him for his dreams because God spoke to him through dreams that his brothers would serve him. And what happened later? He was imprisoned. It looks like punishment, right? After all, his dreams don't make sense.

But what can we see later? The glory of God. He lifted him up as He spoke, and then he became a ruler of all Egypt, and his brothers had to serve him.

Sometimes, God will separate us from some people in times of waiting so He can develop our talents.

God will never send you someone who will take you out of His will but draw you closer to Him.

He will not send you someone with whom you will look good, but someone with whom God will look good.

In **(Matthew 19:6)** Therefore what God has joined together, let not man separate.

What scripture said? What GOD joined together, and not what people joined together.

What God joined together can't be separated simply because there is a purpose to the marriage.

> We are still servants of God, single or married. As wives and husbands, we are one, which means our visions and goals become one also – they must be fully filed for the purpose of marriage according to God's will.
> (1 Peter 4:10-11)

Therefore, in everything will glorify God in Jesus' name

So don't waste time finding your godly man, but prepare yourself and be ready for him – be the best of you.

God is never late – be ready.

Chapter Seven

How do I know my time has come?

- You are healed from your past.
- You do not hide anything from your past.
- You are looking forward and not behind.
- You are teachable.
- Less down selfies
- Submitted minded.
- Focusing on God and His kingdom

1) Definitely you must be healed from any kind of relationship, trauma, or mental or physical abuse from your past.
2) Don't hide anything from your past, which means there is no shame.
3) Looking forward as you are a new creature in Christ, there is a great plan and hope for the new future.
4) Be willing to teach what is good, and so train the young women to love their husbands and children and to be willing to teach from their future husbands.

5) You are no longer selfish; it's not only you anymore, but you are also called to be a servant and helper. You are humble and willing to serve your husband as your king.
6) Willing to submit to your husband as he is submitted to your God.
7) Your priority is to be involved in the Father's business, focusing on His kingdom work and working for God and with God.

If all 7 points are yes, I do, or yes, I am willing, well done, you are ready to meet your king. Remember, never forget your first love, Jesus Christ, who died so you can live forever.

Congratulations, my dear sisters.

We give thanks to you, O, God our Lord, for this learning and growing process. We give you all glory and honour, we thank you, God, for teaching us how to be a woman of God, and we thank you for preparing us for our Kingdom spouse, for a kingdom marriage, to glorify your name in it. As we pray, your will be done in Jesus' name.

Amen

Use this space to thank God for what He does and for what He will do in your life.

Remember waiting patiently as He was waiting for you to come.

Believe in His perfect time; you will meet your husband.

Be always the best of yourself, and prepare; you never know when he will knock on your door.

Dear Father, my Lord, my God_____

Thank you to everyone who purchased this book. I believe you have been blessed.

Also, I would love to invite you to my new FB page, JOYFUL JOURNEY TO MARRIAGE, where we build each other and support each other in times of singleness and in marriage.

Love you all
God bless you.

Copyright © 2021, 2025 Pavla King-Johnson

Published in United Kingdom
by Excel Life Publishing.
All rights reserved.

www.excellifepublishing.com

Author Website:
www.iampkj.com
www.iampkj.company.site

www.ingramcontent.com/pod-product-compliance
Lightning Source LLC
Chambersburg PA
CBHW072122070526
44585CB00016B/1534